CUMBERLAND
AND
WESTMORLAND
COUNTRY RECIPES

COMPILED BY
PIPPA GOMAR

ℛℛ
RAVETTE BOOKS

Published by Ravette Books Limited
3 Glenside Estate, Star Road
Partridge Green, Horsham,
Sussex RH13 8RA
(0403) 710392

Production: Oval Projects Ltd.
Cover design: Jim Wire
Typesetting: Repro-type
Printing & binding: Nørhaven A/S

All recipes are given in Imperial and Metric
weights and measures. Where measurements
are given in 'cups', these are American cups,
holding 8 fluid ounces.

The recipes contained in this book are traditional
and many have been compiled from archival sources.
Every effort has been made to ensure that the recipes
are correct.

RECIPES

SOUPS and BEGINNINGS

FISH

POULTRY and GAME

CAKES, BREADS and BISCUITS

SWEETS and SWEETMEATS

CUMBERLAND AND WESTMORLAND

Cumberland and Westmorland are renowned for the outstanding beauty of the countryside, particularly of the Lake District, famous for Lake Windermere (England's largest lake) and Scarfell Pike (the tallest mountain in England). The region as a whole is especially rich in local customs and traditional dishes, such as Cumberland Rum Nickies, Cumberland Sauce and Kendal Mint Cake.

Many parts of the area are mountainous and, though beautiful and dramatic in appearance, were, and in many places still are, isolated and inaccessible. The farming of sheep for wool and meat has always been a major source of livelihood in these parts. Hence lamb and mutton are a major source of protein and form the basis of dishes such as Westmorland Sweet Pie and Tatie-Pot. Preserving meat was very important in the hilly and mountainous parts.

Until the beginning of this century the sheep were counted in Celtic. Yan, taen, tedderte, medderte, pimp, haata, slaata, lowra, dowra, dick were the numbers from one to ten. Of the breeds of sheep the Herdwick sheep are a very hardy breed suitable for the terrain since they are tolerant of the bad weather conditions and are said to stay on their own 'heaf', meaning that they do not tend to wander away from their grazing area. Beatrix Potter who lived in the Lake District took an interest in this particular breed and was chairman of the Herdwick Sheep Breeder's Association for many years. The sheep are bred for meat and wool, which is rather coarse and suitable for carpets.

'Sheep Meets' have been held for hundreds of years. These occasions allowed shepherds to return wandering sheep to their owners. After their business the shepherds would enjoy Tatie-Pot, apple pie and beer and take part in the famous 'gurning' contests during which prizes were awarded to the shepherd who could pull the worst face!

Game, such as hare, venison and pheasant were commonly caught and eaten. Certain types of game have become have become associated with particular areas: for example, ducks are associated with Derwentwater, pigeons with Crossthwaite, pheasants with Underbarrow and hare with Greystoke.

In the valleys between the mountains, wonderfully clear lakes provide fresh fish. Salmon was so common in the last century that in Kendal one school's rule book stated that boys should not be 'compelled to dine on salmon or fish in general more than 3 days a week'. The renowned char is found in the deepest lakes and special white pottery Char Pots beautifully decorated — some with the fish swimming on them — have for generations been passed down in families.

Sea fish have also played an important part in the creation of what became traditional dishes. Large catches of sea trout, cod and whiting were bought into Cumberland's sea ports, especially Whitehaven, which traded with the West Indies, exchanging wool for ginger, rum, treacle, brown sugar and spices, all of which feature prominently in traditional fare.

Tea in the North of England tends to be a large meal. The local people are particularly fond and proud of their cakes. In addition to the usual cup of tea, cakes, scones and tea cakes, Cumberland Sausage, Cumberland Ham and eggs are often served.

Fruit and vegetables do not grow readily in this part of the country. The most plentiful fruits are sharp tasting varieties of apples and gooseberries. However the Lyth Valley, just south of Windermere, is famous for its beautiful damsons, known locally as Witherslack damsons after the village of that name. It was important to preserve any fruit and vegetables for the winter period. Until the 1930's preserves were exclusively made by the lady of the house in a room, known as the 'stillroom', especially set aside for this important process.

The Mallerstang valley is known for its cheese which is white and crumbly and similar to its better known cousin Wensleydale. The cheese was made almost entirely for home consumption and does not appear to be widespread today.

This lovely area has an abundance of good hotels and restaurants and it is not difficult for the visitor to sample a variety of traditional food of which the local residents are justly proud.

'the loveliest spot that man has ever known'

William Wordsworth

MUTTON BROTH

1 lb (450 g) scrag end of mutton
2 carrots
1 medium turnip
1 large onion
A large pinch of salt
1 oz (25 g) pearl barley
A sprig of parsley
3 pints (1.75 litres/ 7½ cups) water

Put the meat into a large saucepan with the water.

Finely chop the carrots, turnip and onion.

Put the vegetables and the pearl barley into the saucepan with the meat.

Season with a large pinch of salt.

Bring to the boil and simmer gently for 2 hours.

Chop the parsley and add to the broth.

Remove any bones.

Serve hot with brown bread.

HARE SOUP

1 large hare divided into joints
3 small onions
3 cloves
A few blades of mace
A few black peppercorn
½ pint (300 ml/ 1¼ cup) port wine
1½ pints (900 ml/ 3¾ cups) water

Put all the ingredients into a large saucepan.

Bring to the boil, cover and simmer for 1½ hours — 2 hours until the meat is tender.

Strain the soup.

Remove the meat from the bones and return the meat to the soup.

Serve hot.

POTTED CHAR

Char is a member of the salmon family and about the same size as a small trout. It was particularly common and popular around Windermere in the 17th, 18th, and 19th centuries, when it was served for breakfast in a white 'char dish' decorated with pictures of fish.

3 char — each about 6 oz (175 g) in weight
1 small onion, sliced
1 carrot, sliced
¼ pint (150 ml/ ⅔ cup) dry white wine
8 oz (225 g) butter
A few sprigs of parsley
Clarified butter to cover

Clean and scale the fish.

Put the fish, wine, sliced onion, carrot and parsley into a saucepan.

Stew gently over a low heat until the fish is tender.

Take out the fish and then remove the skin and bones.

Put the fish flesh into an earthenware pot.

Melt the butter and pour over the fish.

Bake in a moderate oven for 20-30 minutes.

Completely cover the fish with clarified butter if necessary to seal.

Cool, cover with foil and keep in the refrigerator.

Oven: 350°F/180°C   Gas Mark 4

POTTED SALMON

1 lb (450 g) poached salmon
A pinch of salt
A pinch of cayenne pepper
A pinch of powdered mace
A few drops of anchovy essence
3 oz (75 g) clarified butter
¼ pint (150 ml/ ⅔ cup) double cream

Mash the salmon, salt, cayenne pepper, mace, anchovy essence and cream together.

Beat until smooth.

Press into 6 small ramekins and chill.

Melt the clarified butter and pour over the salmon mixture in each ramekin until covered.

Chill overnight before serving.

POTTED SHRIMPS

1 lb (450 g) cooked shrimps
4 oz (100 g) butter
1 blade of mace
A pinch of cayenne pepper
A pinch of grated nutmeg
2 oz (50 g) clarified butter

Melt the butter with the mace, cayenne pepper and nutmeg.

Stir in the shrimps and heat gently.

Remove the mace.

Pour the mixture into 6 small ramekins.

Cool in the refridgerator.

Melt the clarified butter and pour over the cooled shrimps to cover completely.

Cool again.

Serve with brown bread or toast.

FISH POTTAGE

1 lb (450 g) white fish and eel
2 onions
2 carrots
2 potatoes
2 tablespoons oil
2 pints (1.15 litres/ 5 cups) water or stock made with
   fish trimmings
4 oz (100 g) shrimps
2 tablespoons freshly chopped parsley
A little salt and pepper

Finely chop the onions, carrots and dice the potatoes.

Fry the vegetables in the oil for about 10 minutes.

Cut the fish and eel into 2 inch (5 cm) pieces, removing any
skin and bones.

Put into the pan with the vegetables.

Pour in the water or stock and the chopped parsley.

Bring to the boil and simmer for about 15 minutes.

Add the shrimps, salt and pepper and simmer for another
5 minutes.

Serve hot with bread.

FISH PUDDING

8 oz (225 g) filleted cod or whiting
4 oz (100 g) butter
4 oz (100 g) fresh breadcrumbs
4 tablespoons milk
4 oz (100 g) mushrooms
4 eggs
Salt and pepper
Anchovy sauce

Melt the butter and add the fish.

Stew gently until tender.

Soak the breadcrumbs in the milk.

Mash the fish and breadcrumbs together.

Chop the mushrooms and add to the fish mixture.

Beat the eggs and add.

Season with salt and pepper.

Grease a 1 lb (450 g) loaf tin.

Turn the fish mixture into the tin.

Bake for 30 minutes.

Turn out of the tin and serve with anchovy sauce.

Oven: 400°F/200°C Gas Mark 6

POACHED SALMON

1 salmon — about 4-5 lbs (1.75 - 2.25 kg)
A little salt and pepper

For the court-bouillon:
A few black peppercorns
1 bouquet garni
1 pint (600 ml/ 2½ cups) dry white wine
1 carrot
1 onion
1 teaspoon pickling spice
1 pint (600 ml/ 2½ cups) water

To make the court-bouillon:

Crush the peppercorns.

Slice the carrot and the onion.

Put the crushed peppercorns, bouquet garni, carrot, onion and pickling spice into a saucepan.

Add the wine and the water.

Bring to the boil and simmer, uncovered, for 30 minutes.

Allow to cool.

Wipe the salmon clean and season with salt and pepper.

If you have a fish kettle place the fish on the perforated plate and lower into the kettle. If you do not have a fish kettle put the salmon on a piece of foil that, when doubled over, is a little larger than the bottom of a roasting tin or flameproof dish.

Cover the fish with the court-bouillon.

Poach the fish for 40-50 minutes from the time the liquid just reaches simmering point. It should barely simmer.

Drain well and serve on a warm serving dish, skinned if preferred, with Cucumber Sauce (see recipe).

MARINADED PERCH FILLETS

Serves 4

8 perch fillets
Salt and pepper
2 oz (50 g) flour
2 beaten eggs
6 oz (175 g) stale breadcrumbs
2 tablespoons oil
1 oz (25 g) butter
1 lemon

For the marinade:
1 small onion
Juice of 1 lemon
Salt and pepper
¼ pint (150 ml/ ⅔ cup) oil

To make the marinade:

Chop the onion finely.

Add the onion, lemon juice, salt and pepper to the oil and beat well.

Put the fish fillets in a shallow dish and pour the marinade over.

Leave for at least 1 hour, turning occasionally.

Remove the fillets from the marinade and pat dry.

Roll in flour seasoned with salt and pepper.

Then dip in the beaten egg and finally the breadcrumbs.

Heat the oil and butter in a frying pan and fry the fillets until well brown on both sides.

Serve with lemon wedges.

Rainbow trout fillets may be used instead of perch.

BAKED SALMON TROUT

Serves 6

Salmon trout — about 3 lbs (1.5 kg)
2 oz (50 g) butter
2 oz (50 g) flour
A few sprigs of parsley
A few sprigs of thyme
A few sprigs of tarragon
A little salt and pepper

Clean the fish and wipe dry.

Remove the gut, fins, gills and scales.

Put half of the butter and some of the herbs into the belly of the fish.

Rub the skin with the flour and season with salt and pepper.

Butter a large piece of aluminium foil.

Scatter the remaining herbs on to the foil.

Place the fish in the centre of the foil and wrap it up folding the joined edges twice to seal.

Lay the parcel on a baking tray.

Bake for 30 minutes.

Open the foil and return to the oven for a further 10 minutes to crispen the skin.

Serve with a hollandaise sauce.

Oven: 350°F/180°C Gas Mark 4

BAKED PIKE

In the 18th century the pike was regarded as a noble dish. The roe should not be served as it is very unpleasant.

1 pike — about 3 lbs (1.5 kg)
1 oz (25 g) butter, melted

For the stuffing:
4 oz (100 g) fresh breadcrumbs
1 oz (25 g) butter
1 teaspoon freshly chopped parsley
1 onion
1 egg, beaten

Scale the fish by pouring boiling water over until the scales are dull. Put into cold water and scrape off the scales.

Remove the gut and gills.

Rinse and pat dry inside and outside the fish.

To make the stuffing:

Chop the onion finely.

Melt the butter and add the breadcrumbs, parsley, onion and the beaten egg.

Mix well together and stuff the cavity of the fish.

Sew up with string.

Brush the pike with the melted butter.

Bake for 40-50 minutes. When cooked, the flesh should come away from the bone easily.

Remove the string before serving.

Oven: 350°F/180°C Gas Mark 4

ROAST PHEASANT

1 large pheasant
Salt and freshly ground black pepper
2 oz (50 g) butter
4 oz (100 g) streaky bacon
¾ pint (450 ml/ 2 cups) giblet stock
1 tablespoon flour

For the flavoured butter stuffing:
3 oz (75 g) butter
3 sprigs of watercress
1 tablespoon lemon juice

To make the flavoured butter stuffing:

Beat the butter until pale and creamy.

Chop the watercress, discarding any yellow leaves and tough stalks.

Beat the watercress and the lemon juice into the butter.

Chill.

Wipe the pheasant and sprinkle inside and out with salt and freshly ground black pepper.

Fill the cavity with the chilled flavoured butter.

Truss the bird with skewers and string as you would do a chicken.

Tie the bacon rashers over the breast with string.

Melt the butter in a roasting tin and place the pheasant on top.

Roast for 45 minutes.

Remove the pheasant from the tin and keep hot.

To make the gravy:

Pour any excess fat from the roasting tin, add the flour and cook for a few minutes.

Gradually add the giblet stock and boil for a few minutes until reduced and thickened.

Remove the string and skewers and serve the pheasant decorated with the bird's own tail feathers.

Oven: 400°F/200°C   Gas Mark 6

ROAST GOOSE

Serves 6

Geese were usually kept on country farms for meat, large eggs, and downy feathers to stuff mattresses and pillows. Roast goose has been traditionally served with apple sauce at Christmas time since the 17th century.

The goose fat left over after the roasting was used as a chest rub to treat coughs and bronchitis.

1 oven-ready goose — 8 lbs (3.5 kg)
Salt and freshly ground black pepper

For the stuffing:
4 oz (100 g) fresh breadcrumbs
¼ pint (150 ml/ ⅔ cup) milk
1 cooking apple
2 sticks of celery
Goose liver, chopped
1 large onion
1 tablespoon chopped sage

To make the stuffing:

Soak the breadcrumbs in the milk.

Peel, core and chop the cooking apple.

Finely chop the celery, the goose liver and the onion.

Mix all the stuffing ingredients together and stir in the chopped sage.

To prepare the goose for roasting:

Remove any excess fat and remove the giblets to make giblet stock. You will also need the liver for the stuffing.

Rinse the goose under cold water and dry carefully.

Rub salt and pepper inside the cavity of the goose.

Put the stuffing into the cavity.

Truss the goose with skewers.

Prick the skin all over and rub with salt and pepper.

Place the goose on a rack in a roasting tin.

Roast for 15 minutes at the higher temperature. Reduce the temperature and continue roasting for 2 hours.

20 minutes before the end of the roasting time turn the goose upside down to brown it's back.

The bird is cooked when the juices run clear.

Oven: 425°F/220°C Gas Mark 7
Reduce to: 375°F/190°C Gas Mark 5

GIBLET PIE

For the filling:
1 set of goose giblets
1 lb (450 g) stewing steak
2 onions
1 oz (25 g) flour
Salt and pepper
1 bay leaf

For the pastry:
6 oz (175 g) flour
1½ oz (40 g) butter
1½ oz (40 g) lard
A little cold water
A little milk to glaze

To make the filling:

Cup up the giblets and stewing steak into bite-size pieces.

Season the flour with salt and pepper.

Roll the giblets and stewing steak in the flour.

Place in a pie dish.

Chop the onions and add to the dish.

Add enough water to cover the meat and add the bay leaf.

Cover the pie dish and bake for 2-2½ hours.

To make the pastry:

Rub the butter and lard into the flour until the mixture resembles breadcrumbs.

Add enough cold water to make a soft dough.

Leave to rest for 30 minutes.

Roll out the pastry and place over the pie dish, moistening the edges to seal.

Brush with milk.

Bake for 25 minutes or until the pastry is golden brown, at the higher temperature.

Oven: 375°F/190°C   Gas Mark 5
Increase to: 425°F/220°C   Gas Mark 7

GIBLET STOCK

Giblets from the cavity of an oven-ready bird consist of the neck, gizzard, heart and liver.

Giblets from one bird
1 onion
1 carrot
1 stick of celery
1 bay leaf
A few peppercorns
A pinch of salt
½ pint (300 ml/ 1¼ cups) water

Wash the giblets.

Remove any part that has a greenish tinge.

Put the giblets into a small saucepan.

Slice the onion, carrot and celery.

Add the onion, carrot and celery, a bay leaf, a few peppercorns, a pinch of salt and the water.

Bring to the boil, cover and simmer for 30 minutes.

Strain and cool.

DERWENTWATER DUCKLING

Serves 4

1 duckling — about 4 lbs (1.75 kg)
A little salt and pepper
4 small onions, peeled
4 cloves
4 tablespoons Cumberland Sauce (see recipe)
1 oz (25 g) flour
¼ pint (150 ml/ ⅔ cup) giblet stock
2-3 tablespoons brandy

Wash the duckling and pat dry.

Rub the cavity and the skin with salt and pepper.

Stick a clove into each onion and place the onions into the cavity.

Place the duckling on a rack in a roasting tin.

Roast for 15 minutes at the higher temperature.

Reduce the temperature and roast for a further 1 hour 15 minutes, basting once or twice.

20 minutes before the end of the roasting time turn the duckling upside down to brown it back. The bird is cooked when the juices run clear.

Remove the duckling from the roasting tin and keep warm.

Pour off any excess fat from the tin.

Add the flour to the meaty juices and cook, stirring all the time.

Add the giblet stock, the Cumberland Sauce and brandy.

Simmer for a few minutes.

Serve the duckling with some of the sauce poured over and the remainder served in a sauce boat.

Oven: 425°F/220°C Gas Mark 7
Reduce to: 350°F/180°C Gas Mark 4

ROAST VENISON

3 lbs (1.5 kg) venison — saddle or haunch
4 oz (100 g) butter
1 oz (25 g) flour

For the marinade:
½ pint (300 ml/ 1¼ cups) red wine
1 carrot
1 onion
A sprig of thyme
A bay leaf
1 tablespoon vinegar
2 tablespoons olive oil
1 clove of garlic
1 dessertspoon brown sugar

To make the marinade:

Chop the carrot and the onion.

Boil the wine, carrot, onion, thyme, bay leaf, vinegar, oil, garlic and sugar in a saucepan for 20 minutes. Cool.

Put the venison into the marinade and leave for 24 hours occasionally spooning the marinade over the meat.

Remove the meat from the marinade and place in a roasting tin. Spread the butter over the meat.

Roast for 30 minutes at the higher temperature, then for 1½ hours at the reduced temperature, basting frequently.

Remove the meat from the tin and keep hot.

Add the flour to the fats in the bottom of the tin.

Strain the marinade and gradually stir into the roasting tin.

Simmer for 5 minutes or until the sauce has thickened.

Serve the venison with the marinade sauce.

Oven: 400°F/200°C Gas Mark 6
Reduce to: 350°F/180°C Gas Mark 4

JUGGED HARE

1 large jointed hare
1 tablespoon oil
1 oz (25 g) butter
2 carrots
1 stick of celery
1 onion
A pinch of grounds cloves
Grated rind and juice of 1 lemon
½ pint (300 ml/ 1¼ cups) stock
¼ pint (150 ml/ ⅔ cup) port wine
1 tablespoon redcurrant jelly
1 oz (25 g) butter
1 oz (25 g) flour

For the marinade:
¼ pint (150 ml/ ⅔ cup) red wine
2 tablespoons oil
1 onion
1 carrot
1 bay leaf
Freshly ground black pepper
1 tablespoon vinegar
1 teaspoon brown sugar

To make the marinade:

Chop the onion and carrot.

Mix the wine, oil, onion, carrot, bay leaf, a pinch of black pepper, vinegar and brown sugar together.

Marinade the hare for 6 hours turning occasionally.

Remove the hare and drain well.

Heat the oil and butter in a large flameproof dish and fry the hare to brown on all sides.

Remove from the heat.

Slice the carrots, celery and onion and add to the casserole.

Pour the stock over and season with a pinch of ground cloves, and the grated rind and juice of the lemon.

Strain the marinade and pour it into the casserole.

Cover and cook for 2½-3 hours or until the meat is tender.

Remove the hare and keep warm in a clean flameproof dish.

Add the port and the redcurrant jelly to the stock in the casserole dish and cook over a low heat.

Mix the butter and flour together and gradually add to the liquid.

Cook until thickened slightly.

Pour over the hare and serve.

Oven: 350°F/180°C   Gas Mark 4

ROAST LAMB

1 leg of lamb — about 3 lbs (1.5 kg)
2 oz (50 g) butter
Salt and pepper
1 garlic clove
2 tablespoons freshly chopped parsley
4 oz (100 g) breadcrumbs
1 tablespoon flour
½ pint (300 ml/ 1¼ cups) stock

Melt the butter in a roasting tin on the top of the oven.

Brown the lamb on all sides to seal in the juices.

Sprinkle the meat with salt and pepper.

Roast in the oven for about 1½ hours.

Crush the garlic clove.

Mix the garlic, parsley and breadcrumbs together.

Coat the lamb with the mixture and return to the oven at the higher temperature for 10 minutes until it is golden brown.

Make a gravy from the meaty juices in the roasting tin by adding a tablespoon flour, mixing well and gradually adding ½ pint (300 ml/ 1¼ cups) stock.

Simmer until thick and smooth, stirring all the time.

Oven: 375°F/190°C Gas Mark 5
Raise to: 400°F/200°C Gas Mark 6

LAMB'S LIVER AND ONIONS

1 lb (450 g) lamb's liver
1 oz (25 g) flour
Salt and freshly ground black pepper
2 tablespoons oil
1 oz (25 g) butter
A little chopped parsley
1 lemon
1 lb (450 g) onions

Slice the onions thinly.

Heat 1 tablespoon oil and half of the butter in a pan.

Add the onions and fry gently until soft and golden, keeping the pan covered.

Stir from time to time.

Wash the liver and pat dry.

Thinly slice the liver lengthwise, cutting out any gristle or veins.

Remove any skin.

Season the flour with salt and pepper.

Toss the liver in the flour until well coated.

Remove the onions from the pan and keep warm.

Heat the remaining oil and butter and quickly fry the liver for a few minutes.

Return the onions to the pan and cook gently until the liver is tender, adding a little hot water if necessary to prevent the bottom of the pan burning.

Serve with parsley and lemon wedges.

MUTTON CHOPS WITH MINT AND PARSLEY

Serves 4

4 mutton or lamb chops
2 oz (50 g) butter
2 tablespoons chopped mint
2 tablespoons chopped parsley
A little oil

Beat the butter and herbs together.

Cut a slit in the meaty part of the each chop and stuff with the herb mixture.

Brush the chops with a little oil and grill for about 8 minutes on each side.

Garnish with more mint and parsley and serve with mashed potato.

MUTTON HOT POT

Serves 4

4 lean mutton chops
4 large onions
8 carrots
8 large potatoes
Salt and pepper
1 oz (25 g) flour
2 oz (50 g) butter
A pinch of thyme
1 dessertspoonful brown sugar
1 pint (600 ml/ 2½ cups) stock

Rub the salt and pepper into the mutton chops.

Roll each one in flour.

Brown the chops on all sides in the butter.

Place in a large casserole dish.

Slice the onions, carrots and potatoes.

Gently fry the onions and carrots until barely soft.

Add these to the casserole.

Sprinkle with the thyme and the brown sugar.

Arrange the sliced potatoes on top of the meat and vegetables.

Pour the stock over.

Cover and cook for 2 hours.

After 1½ hours remove the lid and return to the oven for 30 minutes to brown the potatoes.

Oven: 325°F/160°C Gas Mark 3

CUMBERLAND SWEET PIE

6 oz (175 g) puff pastry
8 oz (225 g) mutton
1 lb 12 oz (800 g) mixed dried fruit
4 oz (100 g) soft brown sugar
Juice of 1 lemon
A pinch of ground cinnamon
A pinch of ground mace
A pinch of grated nutmeg
A little salt and pepper
A little milk to glaze

Mince the mutton and mix with the dried fruit, sugar, lemon juice, cinnamon, mace and nutmeg.

Season with salt and pepper.

Put into a pie dish.

Roll out the pastry.

Cover the dish with the pastry.

Brush with milk to glaze.

Bake for 30 minutes.

Oven: 400°F/200°C Gas Mark 6

CUMBERLAND TATIE-POT

Serves 4

1½ lbs (675 g) potatoes
2 onions
8 oz (225 g) carrots
1 small turnip
1 pint (600 ml/ 2½ cups) stock
1 lb (450 g) mutton
1 black pudding
A little salt and pepper

Remove any excess fat from the mutton and cut into cubes.

Slice the black pudding.

Put the meat and black pudding into a casserole dish.

Slice the carrots, onions and turnip.

Add to the casserole.

Pour the stock over.

Season with salt and pepper.

Thickly slice the potatoes and arrange on top of the ingredients in the casserole dish.

Cook for 2-3 hours until the potatoes are tender and golden brown.

Serve with Pickled Red Cabbage (see recipe).

Oven: 350°F/180°C Gas Mark 4

WESTMORLAND SWEET PIE

This savoury pie was an important part of traditional Christmas fare.

For the pastry:
12 oz (350 g) flour
3 oz (75 g) butter
3 oz (75 g) lard
A little water
A little milk to glaze

For the filling:
8 oz (225 g) lamb
1½ lb (675 g) mixed dried fruit
4 oz (100 g) soft brown sugar
4 tablespoons rum
A large pinch of ground mace
A large pinch of grated nutmeg
A large pinch of ground cinnamon
A little salt and black pepper

To make the pastry:

Rub the butter and lard into the flour until the mixture resembles breadcrumbs.

Add enough water to make a soft dough.

Leave for 30 minutes.

To make the filling:

Mince the lamb and mix with the mixed dried fruit.

Add the sugar, rum, mace, nutmeg and cinnamon.

Season with salt and black pepper.

Divide the pastry into two halves.

Roll out one half and line a large shallow pie dish.

Pile the filling on to the pastry base.

Roll out the remaining pastry to cover the filling, moistening then crimping the edges of the pastry to seal.

Prick the crust with a fork and brush with milk.

Bake for 30 minutes.

Oven: 400°F/200°C Gas Mark 6

CUMBERLAND SAUSAGES

Cumberland sausage is traditionally made in long lengths.

5 lbs (2.25 kg) pork (boned)
A pinch of sage
A pinch of marjoram
1 teaspoonful of white pepper
2 oz (50 g) salt
Sausage casings

Mince the meat.

Add the sage, marjoram, salt and pepper.

Mix well.

Fill the sausage casings and twist at intervals.

Prick well with a fork.

Place, coiled up, in a roasting tin, in the oven.

Cook for 30 minutes until well brown all over, turning once during cooking.

Serve with Apple Sauce (see recipe).

Oven: 350°F/180°C Gas Mark 4

CUMBERLAND HAM

1 ham — about 10 lbs (4.5 kg)
Juice of ½ lemon
2 oz (50 g) dried breadcrumbs
1 oz (25 g) soft brown sugar
1 teaspoon made-up English mustard

Soak the ham overnight in cold water.

Scrape the skin.

Put the ham into a large saucepan with the lemon juice and cover with cold water.

Bring to the boil and simmer for 3 hours 40 minutes.

Remove the ham from the water. The stock may be used for soups.

Strip off the skin and mark a diamond pattern on the fat underneath.

Mix the breadcrumbs, sugar and mustard and spread this over the ham.

Serve with Cumberland Sauce (see recipe), or cover with tin foil and place in a roasting tin.

Pour ¼ pint (150 ml/ ⅔ cup) of the ham stock into the tin and roast in a hot oven for about 30 minutes.

Oven: 425°F/220°C   Gas Mark 7

The ham may be baked instead of boiled, covered with foil.

Bake for 15 minutes at the higher temperature and then for 5 hours at the reduced temperature.

Oven: 375°F/190°C   Gas Mark 5
Reduce to: 325°F/160°C   Gas Mark 3

POTATO PASTIES

Makes 4

For the pastry:
12 oz (350 g) flour
3 oz (75 g) lard
3 oz (75 g) butter
A little cold water
Milk to glaze

For the filling:
1 onion
2 large potatoes
8 oz (225 g) minced lamb or beef
Salt and pepper
½ teaspoon dried parsley

To make the pastry:

Rub the butter and lard into the flour until the mixture resembles breadcrumbs.

Add enough cold water to make a soft dough.

Leave for 30 minutes.

To make the filling:

Finely chop the onion.

Peel and dice the potatoes into very small cubes.

Mix the onion, potato, minced meat and dried parsley.

Season with salt and pepper.

Roll out the pastry and cut into 4 circles each the size of a small saucepan lid.

Divide the filling equally between the pastry circles, placing it in the centre of each circle.

Moisten the edes of the pastry, fold over and press firmly together, crimping the edges with your fingers.

Brush each pasty with milk.

Bake on a greased baking tray for 15 minutes at the higher oven temperature.

Reduce the temperature and bake for a further 45 minutes.

Oven: 425°F/220°F Gas Mark 7
Reduce to: 350°F/180°C Gas Mark 4

EASTER LEDGE PUDDING

This was traditionally served at Easter time when the plants used would be young and green and there was very little edible green food in the garden. Easter Ledges or Bistort grow wild in the hay meadows of the Lake District.

12 oz (350 g) young Bistorts
4 oz (100 g) young nettle tops
1 large onion
4 oz (100 g) pot barley
½ teaspoon salt
1 egg
1 oz (25 g) butter
A little black pepper

Chop the Bistorts, nettle tops and onions.

Add the barley and salt.

Toss to combine well.

Boil in a muslin bag for about 2 hours.

Just before serving, beat the mixture with 1 egg and half of the butter.

Season with black pepper.

Make into a flat patty and fry in the remaining butter.

Serve with bacon and eggs, lamb or veal.

Wheat Sheaf

PEASE PUDDING

This 'pudding' has been traditionally served with pork since the Middle Ages.

8 oz (225 g) dried peas
1 bouquet garni
1 egg
2 oz (50 g) butter
A little salt and pepper

Soak the peas in water overnight.

Drain the peas, rinse thoroughly and drain again.

Put them with the bouquet garni in a saucepan and cover with plenty of fresh water.

Boil for 1-1½ hours until soft.

Remove the bouquet garni.

Blend the peas to a purée or rub them through a wire-meshed sieve.

Beat in the butter and egg.

Season with a little salt and pepper.

Turn into a greased pie dish and bake for 30 minutes.

Oven: 350°F/180°C Gas Mark 4

Barrow

BAKED ONIONS

Serves 4 as an accompaniment to a meal

4 medium onions
1 oz (25 g) lard
A little salt and pepper

Wash the onions but do not peel them.

Melt the lard and brush it over the onions.

Bake for 1 hour or until tender.

Season with salt and pepper.

Oven: 350°F/180°C   Gas Mark 4

HOT RED CABBAGE

This vegetable is traditionally served with venison and game.

1 red cabbage
2 cooking apples
1 tablespoon brown sugar
A few cloves
1 onion
1 pint (600 ml/ 2½ cups) water
A pinch of salt and pepper
4 tablespoons red wine

Shred the cabbage discarding the core.

Peel, core and slice the apples.

Chop the onion.

Put the cabbage, apple, and onion into a large saucepan with the sugar, cloves, salt, pepper, red wine and water.

Bring to the boil and cover.

Simmer gently for 2 hours.

Strain.

Serve hot.

HASTY PUDDING

Serves 3-4

This dish is mentioned in Dorothy Wordsworth's diary. There are many variations of Hasty Pudding though it was always made of oatmeal. It was eaten at breakfast and often at supper.

1 pint (600 ml/ 2½ cups) milk
8 oz (225 g) oatmeal
1 egg yolk
A pinch of salt
2 oz (50 g) soft brown sugar
1 oz (25 g) butter or a little cream

Mix the oatmeal, salt, egg yolk and sugar with a little of the milk.

Heat the remaining milk.

Just before the milk boils add the oatmeal mixture.

Boil for a few minutes until thick, stirring all the time.

Serve hot, dotted with butter or with cream.

CONISTON PUDDING

For the pastry:
6 oz (175 g) flour
3 oz (75 g) butter
1 oz (25 g) caster sugar
1 egg

For the filling:
1 egg
1 oz (25 g) caster sugar
A pinch of grated nutmeg
¼ pint (150 ml/ ⅔ cup) hot milk/single cream mixture
1 oz (25 g) raisins
1 oz (25 g) currants
½ oz (15 g) chopped candied peel

To make the pastry:

Rub the butter into the flour until the mixture resembles breadcrumbs.

Add the sugar and mix well.

Beat the egg and mix in to make a soft dough.

Leave for 30 minutes to rest.

Roll out and line an 8 inch (20 cm) flan dish with it.

To make the filling:

Beat the egg and add the sugar and grated nutmeg.

Add the hot milk/cream, the raisins, currants and candied peel.

Mix well.

Pour into the pastry case.

Bake for 50 minutes.

Oven: 350°F/180°C   Gas Mark 4

LAMPLUGH PUDDING

This pudding was made for the farmers who had been out for long periods in bitterly cold weather especially at lambing time. It was also served at Christmas.

1 pint (600 ml/ 2½ cups) brown ale
A pinch of ground cloves
A pinch of ground allspice
A pinch of ground cinnamon
2 oz (50 g) soft brown sugar
8 oz (225 g) rolled oats
8 oz (225 g) raisins
Grated rind and juice of 1 lemon
4 sweet biscuits

Boil the ale with ground cloves, allspice and cinnamon for 5 minutes.

Remove from the heat.

Add the sugar, oats, raisins, lemon rind and juice.

Serve hot in bowls with lightly crushed sweet biscuits sprinkled on top.

CUMBERLAND APPLE PUDDING   Serves 4

6 oz (175 g) cooking apples
4 oz (100 g) fresh white breadcrumbs
3 oz (75 g) shredded suet
1 teaspoon baking powder
2 oz (50 g) flour
3 oz (75 g) caster sugar or to taste
A pinch of grated nutmeg
1 tablespoon golden syrup
2 eggs
4-6 tablespoons milk
Grated rind of lemon

Mix the breadcrumbs, suet, baking powder, flour, sugar and grated nutmeg together.

Warm the golden syrup.

Beat the eggs, the golden syrup and the grated lemon rind together and add to the dry ingredients.

Peel, core and grate the apples and add to the mixture.

Add enough milk to make a soft dough.

Turn the dough into a lightly greased 2 pint (1.15 litre) pudding basin.

Cover with foil, tie down and steam in a saucepan of boiling water for 2½ hours, topping up with water if necessary.

Turn out while still hot and serve with cream, custard or Apple Sauce (see recipe).

APPLE PIE

For the pastry:
12 oz (350 g) flour
3 oz (75 g) butter
3 oz (75 g) lard
A little cold water
A little milk to glaze

For the filling:
1½ lb (675 g) cooking apples
2 oz (50 g) sugar or to taste
Grated rind of ½ lemon
Caster sugar to coat

To make the pastry:

Rub the butter and lard into the flour until the mixture resembles breadcrumbs.

Add enough cold water to make a soft dough.

Leave to rest for 30 minutes.

To make the filling:

Peel, core and slice the apples.

Simmer in a saucepan with the grated lemon rind and the barest minimum of water, until only just soft.

Allow to cool.

Divide the pastry into two halves.

Roll out one half and line a 2 pint (1.15 litre) pie dish.

Fill the pastry case with the apples and sprinkle with the sugar.

Roll out the remaining pastry and cover the filling, moistening the edges of the pastry to seal.

Prick the pastry lid all over with a fork and brush with milk.

Bake for 30 minutes or until golden brown.

Serve dusted with caster sugar and cream separately.

Oven: 400°F/200°C Gas Mark 6

WESTMORLAND THREE DECKERS

12 oz (350 g) flour
A pinch of salt
6 oz (175 g) butter
A little cold water
1 lb (450 g) plums
2 oz (50 g) caster sugar
A little milk to glaze

Sift the flour and salt.

Rub in the flour until the mixture resembles breadcrumbs.

Add enough cold water to make a soft dough.

Leave to rest for 30 minutes.

Divide the dough into three pieces of equal size.

Roll out one piece and line a pie plate.

Put half of the plums on to the dough.

Sprinkle with half of the sugar.

Roll out the second piece of dough and place over the fruit.

Put the remaining plums on top and sprinkle with the remaining sugar.

Roll out the third piece of dough and place over the fruit.

Brush the pastry with milk to glaze.

Bake for 1 hour.

Serve with cream and a little extra sugar.

Oven: 375°F/190°C Gas Mark 5

GOOSEBERRY PIE

Serves 4-6

6 oz (175 g) puff pastry
1½ lb (675 g) gooseberries
4 oz (100 g) caster sugar
Milk to glaze

Top and tail the gooseberries.

Put the gooseberries into a buttered 2 pint (1.15 litre) pie dish.

Sprinkle with the sugar.

Roll out the pastry.

Moisten the edges of the dish and lay the pastry over the filling.

Brush the pastry with the milk to glaze.

Bake for 30-40 minutes.

Serve with cream or custard.

Oven: 400°F/200°C Gas Mark 6

RASPBERRY FOOL

This is an 18th century recipe.

1 pint (600 ml/ 2½ cups) raspberries
2 tablespoon orange-flower water
5 oz (150 g) caster sugar
1 pint (600 ml/ 2½ cups) single cream

Strain the raspberries through a fine mesh wire sieve to remove the pips.

Add the orange-flower water to the raspberry pulp.

Add the sugar.

Bring the cream to the boil and add the juices.

Stir once, pour into a basin and leave to cool.

BAKED APPLES

Serves 4

4 cooking apples
A little water
8 oz (225 g) rum butter (see recipe)
2 oz (50 g) raisins

Wash and core the apples.

Make a cut in the skin around the middle of each apple.

Beat the raisins into the rum butter.

Fill the centres of the apples with rum butter and pile the remainder on top of each apple.

Place the apples in an ovenproof dish.

Pour a little water to cover the bottom of the dish.

Bake for about 30 minutes, basting once or twice with the juices from the bottom of the dish.

Serve hot with cream.

Oven: 350°F/180°C Gas Mark 4

RICE PUDDING

4 oz (100 g) pudding rice
1 pint (600 ml/ 2½ cups) milk
2 oz (50 g) butter
3 eggs
1 tablespoon brandy
1 tablespoon of rose-water
A pinch of grated nutmeg
2 oz (50 g) caster sugar

Melt the butter in the milk over a low heat.

Add the rice and bring to the boil.

Simmer gently until the rice is tender.

Leave to cool.

Stir in the eggs.

When the mixture is cold add the brandy, nutmeg, grated rose-water and sugar.

CUMBERLAND PUDDING

Serves 4

4 oz (100 g) flour
3 oz (75 g) caster sugar
2 oz (50 g) butter
2 eggs
A pinch of salt
2 pints (1.15 litres/ 5 cups) milk
Grated rind of 1 lemon

Melt the butter over a low heat.

Add the flour and sugar, eggs, salt and lemon rind.

Beat with a little of the milk until smooth.

Boil the rest of the milk and add to the mixture.

Pour into a buttered large dish.

Bake for 30 minutes.

Oven: 350°F/180°C Gas Mark 4

CUMBERLAND CAKE

Serves 6-8

For the pastry:
8 oz (225 g) flour
4 oz (100 g) butter
1 oz (25 g) caster sugar
1 egg

For the filling:
1 oz (25 g) butter
2 oz (50 g) soft brown sugar
8 oz (225 g) mixed dried fruit
1 tablespoon lemon juice

For the topping:
1 egg white
1 oz (25 g) caster sugar

To make the pastry:

Rub the butter into the flour until the mixture resembles breadcrumbs.

Add the sugar.

Beat the egg and add to bind the pastry.

Leave to rest for 30 minutes.

Roll out half of the pastry and line an 8 inch (20 cm) flan dish or pie dish.

To make the filling:

Melt the butter and add the sugar, dried fruit and lemon juice.

Pile the mixture on to the pastry base.

Roll out the remaining pastry and place over the filling moistening the edges to seal.

Bake for 30 minutes or until the pastry is a pale golden brown.

To make the topping:

Whisk the egg white until stiff.

Add half of the sugar and whisk again until stiff.

Fold in the remaining sugar.

Spread the meringue mixture over the top of the pie.

Return to the oven until the meringue has set.

Serve warm.

Oven: 400°F/200°C   Gas Mark 6

DAMSON COBBLER

Serves 6

For the damson filling:
2 lb (1 kg) damsons
4 oz (100 g) sugar or to taste
A little water

For the scone topping:
8 oz (225 g) self-raising flour
2 oz (50 g) butter
2 oz (50 g) caster sugar
A little milk

To make the filling:

Put the damsons into a large saucepan with the sugar and a little water.

Heat gently until the damsons are soft.

Remove the stones.

Turn the damsons into an ovenproof dish.

To make the topping:

Sieve the flour and rub in the butter.

Add the sugar.

Gradually pour in enough milk to make a soft dough.

Roll out the dough on a floured surface to a thickness of ½ inch (1 cm).

Cut out small circles with a pastry cutter.

Place the scones overlapping each other in a circle on top of the damsons.

Brush the scones with milk to glaze.

Bake for about 20 minutes or until the scone topping is brown and well risen.

Oven: 400°F/200°C Gas Mark 6

WESTMORLAND CREAM PANCAKES

8 oz (225 g) flour
1 level teaspoon bicarbonate of soda
1 level teaspoon cream of tartar
A pinch of salt
¼ pint (150 ml/ ⅔ cup) single cream
¼ pint (150 ml/ ⅔ cup) milk

Mix the milk and cream together.

Dissolve the bicarbonate of soda and cream of tartar in the milk and cream mixture.

Gradually add to the flour beating all the time.

Season with salt.

Pour a little of the pancake mixture into a greased and heated frying pan.

Turn each pancake over when one side is cooked and lightly brown.

You can make large or small pancakes with the mixture.

SAUCER PANCAKES

2 oz (50 g) butter
2 oz (50 g) caster sugar
2 eggs
2 oz (50 g) flour
½ pint (300 ml/ 1¼ cups) milk
Icing sugar to coat

Grease 4 ovenproof saucers.

Cream together the butter and sugar until pale and fluffy.

Beat the eggs.

Gradually add the eggs and the flour to the butter and sugar.

Gradually beat in the milk.

Beat until the batter is smooth.

Leave to rest for 30 minutes.

Pour the mixture on to the saucers and leave for another 30 minutes.

Bake for 10-15 minutes until firm.

Fold each pancake in half and sprinkle with icing sugar.

Serve with jam.

Oven: 350°F/180°C Gas Mark 4

DROP CAKES

8 oz (225 g) flour
4 oz (100 g) butter
2 oz (50 g) caster sugar
4 oz (100 g) currants
1 egg
A tablespoon of brandy
A little rose-water

Rub the flour and butter together until the mixture resembles breadcrumbs.

Mix in the sugar and currants.

Beat the egg and add.

Add the brandy and enough rose-water to make a soft 'dropping' batter.

Drop the mixture in spoonfuls on to a lightly greased hot griddle or frying pan.

Cook on both sides.

Serve hot with butter.

GRASMERE GINGERBREAD

Gingerbread made to the special recipe of a local woman, Sarah Nelson, is still baked in a small shop in Grasmere near Dove Cottage, the home at one time of Dorothy and William Wordsworth. It is crisp and biscuit-like. The original recipe is a closely guarded secret, but this gingerbread is similar.

8 oz (225 g) oatmeal
2 teaspoons ground ginger
½ teaspoon bicarbonate of soda
½ teaspoon cream of tartar
1 tablespoon golden syrup
6 oz (175 g) soft brown sugar
4 oz (100 g) butter

Mix the oatmeal, ginger, bicarbonate of soda and cream of tartar together.

Melt the syrup, butter and sugar together over a gentle heat.

Add to the dry ingredients, stirring to combine well.

Grease an 8 inch (20 cm) shallow tin.

Press the gingerbread mixture into the tin.

Bake for about 45 minutes.

Mark the gingerbread into squares then leave in the tin until cold.

Oven: 325°F/160°C Gas Mark 3

GINGER SCONES

8 oz (225 g) flour
1 teaspoon bicarbonate of soda
1 teaspoon cream of tartar
2 oz (50 g) butter
1 oz (25 g) caster sugar
1 tablespoon golden syrup
2 teaspoons ground ginger
1 egg
A little milk

Rub the butter into the flour.

Add the bicarbonate of soda, cream of tartar, sugar and ground ginger.

Warm the golden syrup and beat in the egg.

Mix into the dry ingredients.

Add a little milk if necessary to make a soft dough.

Roll out the dough to a thickness of ½ inch (1 cm).

Cut out circles or triangles.

Place the scones on a greased baking tray.

Brush with milk to glaze.

Bake for 10-15 minutes.

Serve hot with butter.

Oven: 400°F/200°C Gas Mark 6

PARKIN

1 lb (450 g) medium oatmeal
8 oz (225 g) flour
1 lb (450 g) treacle
1 teaspoon bicarbonate of soda
8 oz (225 g) butter
8 oz (225 g) soft brown sugar
2 teaspoons ground ginger
About ¼ pint (150 ml/ ⅔ cup) milk

Seive together the flour, bicarbonate of soda and ground ginger.

Add the oatmeal.

Melt the butter, treacle and sugar and add to the dry ingredients.

Stir in enough milk to make a soft mixture.

Grease a square tin. Line it with greaseproof paper and grease again.

Turn the mixture into the tin.

Bake for 1½ hours.

Leave in the tin for 24 hours then cut into squares.

Oven: 325°F/160°C   Gas Mark 3

WESTMORLAND PEPPER CAKE

This cake was once as important at Christmas time in Westmorland as rich fruit cake is today. It was customary to offer it to the carol singers who came around.

2 lbs (1 kg) flour
2 teaspoons baking powder
1 lb (450 g) caster sugar
1 lb (450 g) treacle
8 oz (225 g) butter
1 lb (450 g) mixed dried fruit
1 oz (25 g) ground ginger
½ teaspoon black pepper
3 eggs

Mix the flour and the baking powder together.

Rub in the butter.

Add the sugar, mixed dried fruit, ginger and pepper.

Beat the eggs and treacle together.

Add to the rest of the ingredients.

Pour into a greased 8 inch (20 cm) cake tin.

Bake for 1 hour.

Oven: 325°F/160°C Gas Mark 3

CUMBERLAND BUTTERMILK CAKE

1 lb (450 g) flour
2 oz (50 g) lard
4 oz (100 g) unsalted butter
4 oz (100 g) caster sugar
8 oz (225 g) chopped candied lemon peel
Grated rind of 1 lemon
6 oz (175 g) raisins
2 tablespoons marmalade
1 teaspoon bicarbonate of soda
½ pint (300 ml/ 1¼ cups) buttermilk

Sift the flour and rub in the lard and butter.

Stir in the sugar, candied lemon peel, grated lemon rind and the raisins.

Heat the buttermilk gently and stir in the marmalade.

Leave to cool a little, then add the bicarbonate of soda.

Stir the liquid into the dry ingredients to make a soft dough.

Turn the mixture into a greased and lined 8 inch (20 cm) round cake tin.

Bake for 2 hours.

Serve cold.

Oven: 300°F/150°C Gas Mark 2

CUMBERLAND NICKIES

For the pastry:
8 oz (225 g) flour
4 oz (100 g) butter
A pinch of salt
A little cold water

For the filling:
4 oz (100 g) currants
1 oz (25 g) brown sugar
A large pinch of grated nutmeg
1 oz (25 g) butter
1 tablespoon rum

To make the pastry:

Rub the butter into the flour until the mixture resembles breadcrumbs.

Add a pinch of salt.

Mix to a soft dough with a little cold water.

Leave to rest for 30 minutes then roll out and cut into 3 inch (7.5 cm) diameter circle.

To make the filling:

Melt the butter.

Add the rum and nutmeg.

Add the sugar and currants and leave for about an hour.

Place a little filling on to half of the pastry circles.

Cover with the remaining pastry circles, moistening the edges to seal.

Prick the top of each Nicky with a fork.

Bake for 10-15 minutes.

Oven: 400°F/200°C Gas Mark 6

WINDERMERE SPICE BISCUITS

Makes about 40 biscuits

8 oz (225 g) butter
8 oz (225 g) soft brown sugar
12 oz (350 g) self-raising flour
1-2 teaspoons caraway seeds
1 teaspoon cinnamon
2 eggs

Cream the butter and sugar.

Add the flour, caraway seeds and cinnamon.

Beat the eggs and add gradually to the biscuit mixture.

Knead the dough until smooth.

Roll out to a thickness of ½ inch (1 cm).

Cut into small circles with a pastry cutter.

Bake for 20-30 minutes.

Cool on a wire rack.

Oven: 350°F/180°C Gas Mark 4

HAWKSHEAD BISCUITS

1 lb (450 g) self-raising flour
4 oz (100 g) butter
1 oz (25 g) caster sugar
1 egg
½ pint (300 ml/ 1¼ cups) milk
A pinch of salt
Grated rind of 1 lemon

Rub the butter into the flour.

Add the sugar and salt.

Mix in the grated lemon rind.

Beat the egg and milk together and gradually add to the dry ingredients to make a soft dough.

Divide the dough into 8 pieces.

Roll out each piece to a circle with a thickness of ½ inch (1 cm).

Prick each biscuit with a fork.

Place on a greased baking sheet.

Bake for about 15 minutes.

Cool on a wire rack.

Oven: 350°F/180°C Gas Mark 4

KENDAL WIGS

1 lb (450 g) flour
1½ oz (40 g) lard
1½ oz (40 g) soft brown sugar
1 oz (25 g) fresh yeast
A little warm water
A pinch of salt
1 oz (25g) currants
Rum butter

Warm the water to a hand-hot temperature.

Dissolve the sugar in the warm water.

Sprinkle in the yeast and leave for ten minutes or until the mixture is frothy.

Rub the lard into the flour.

Add a pinch of salt.

Pour in the yeast mixture and mix to a soft dough, adding a little milk if necessary.

Knead for 10 minutes or until the dough is smooth and elastic.

Knead in the currants.

Put the dough into a greased polythene bag or into a greased bowl covered with a damp cloth.

Leave in warm place until the dough has doubled in size.

Divide the mixture into about 20 small pieces and shape into buns.

Place these, well spaced out, on greased baking sheets.

Leave to rise again.

Bake for 15 minutes.

Serve warm with Rum butter (see recipe).

Oven: 400°F/200°C   Gas Mark 6

OATCAKES

Makes about 25

4 oz (100 g) flour
4 oz (100 g) rolled oats
1 oz (25 g) caster sugar
2 oz (50 g) butter
1 oz (25 g) lard
A pinch of salt
½ teaspoon bicarbonate of soda
1 tablespoon water
A little milk

Sieve the flour into a bowl

Add the rolled oats, sugar and salt.

Melt the butter, lard, bicarbonate of soda and water in a small saucepan.

Add to the dry ingredients and beat well.

Add enough milk to make a firm dough.

Roll the dough out to a thickness of ¼ inch (5 mm).

Cut out small circles with a pastry cutter.

Place, well spaced out, on a greased baking sheet.

Bake for about 15 minutes or until pale golden brown.

Cool and serve with soft cheese.

Oven: 375°F/190°C Gas Mark

HAVVER BREAD/CLAP BREAD

This bread was always made of oatmeal. The name 'havver' comes from the old Norse word 'hafrar' meaning oats, while the name Clap is derived from the preparation of the bread which was clapped or beaten with the hand into a wide, thin bread.

6 oz (175 g) oatmeal
2 oz (50 g) wholewheat flour
A pinch of salt
A pinch of bicarbonate of soda
1 tablespoon melted dripping
Boiling water

Mix the oatmeal, flour, salt and bicarbonate of soda.

Add the melted dripping and mix well.

Pour in enough boiling water to make a dough.

Knead the dough well on a floured surface.

Roll it out thinly and cut into circles or triangles.

Cook for about 25 minutes until crisp and brown.

Cool on a wire rack.

Serve with cheese, jam or paté.

Oven: 350°F/180°C Gas Mark 4

SODA CAKE

1 lb (450 g) flour
8 oz (225 g) butter
8 oz (225 g) caster sugar
8 oz (225 g) currants
8 oz (225 g) sultanas
A pinch of salt
2 teaspoons bicarbonate of soda
¼ pint (150 ml/ ⅔ cup) milk
2 eggs

Rub the butter into the flour until the mixture resembles breadcrumbs.

Add the sugar, dried fruit and salt.

Mix well.

Dissolve the bicarbonate of soda in the milk, beat in the eggs and mix into the dry ingredients.

Put into a 8 inch (20 cm) cake tin.

Bake for 1½ to 2 hours.

Oven: 350°F/180°C Gas Mark 4

KENDAL MINT CAKE

This sweetmeat has been taken on many mountaineering expeditions, most notably on the Mount Everest ascent by Sir Edmund Hillary and Sirdar Tensing.

1 lb (450 g) white or soft brown sugar
1 teaspoon peppermint essence or ½ teaspoon oil of peppermint
¼ pint (150 ml/ ⅔ cup) milk

Put the milk and sugar into a saucepan.

Boil until the soft ball stage is reached at a temperature of 240°F/115°C.

Remove from the heat and add the peppermint essence or oil of peppermint.

Beat until the mixture is smooth and beginning to set.

Pour into a greased tin to a depth of about ¼ inch (5 mm).

Mark into squares just before it sets.

TREACLE TOFFEE

This toffee may also be used to coat apples for making toffee apples.

1 lb (450 g) soft brown sugar
4 oz (100 g) treacle
4 oz (100 g) butter
1 tablespoon milk
1 tablespoon water
1 tablespoon vinegar

Put the sugar, treacle, butter, milk and water into a saucepan.

Boil for about 20 minutes until the temperature of the mixture reaches 275°F/140°C.

If you do not have a thermometer drop a little of the mixture into cold water. If it hardens to a brittle toffee, it is ready.

Stir in the vinegar.

Pour into a shallow greased tin.

Score into small squares before it is set.

DAMSON CHEESE

Makes about 2 lb (1 kg)

This cheese is traditionally served alongside port wine and with cream poured over it.

2 lb (1 kg) damsons
About 1 lb (450 g) granulated sugar
A little brandy

Put the damsons into an ovenproof dish.

Cook in a low oven for 20-30 minutes until the fruit is tender.

Put the fruit through a wire meshed sieve.

Measure the pulp.

To every pint (600 ml/ 2½ cups) of pulp add 1 lb (450 g) sugar.

Crack the damson stones and add the kernels to the pulp and sugar.

In a saucepan warm the mixture until the sugar has dissolved.

Bring to the boil and boil until the mixture has thickened.

Turn into warm, sterilized jars.

Place a circle of greaseproof paper soaked in brandy on top of the damson cheese.

Cool and seal.

The cheese improves with time so keep for at least 6 months in a cool place before using.

Oven: 300°F/150°C Gas Mark 2

GOOSEBERRY MARMALADE

Makes about 3 lb (1.5 kg)

2 lbs (1 kg) gooseberries
2 lbs (1 kg) granulated sugar
2 pints (1.15 litres/ 5 cups) water
Grated rind and juice of 1 lemon

Top and tail the gooseberries.

Put into a large saucepan with the sugar, water, and grated rind and juice of the lemon.

Bring to the boil and boil for 1 hour or until setting point has been reached.

To test for setting point put a teaspoonful of marmalade on to a cold plate. If the mixture forms a skin that wrinkles when touched, setting point has been reached.

Pour into warm, sterilized jars.

When cold cover with a circle of greaseproof paper and a lid.

Store in a cool place.

DAMSON JAM

Makes about 3 lbs (1.5 kg)

2 lbs (1 kg) damsons
2 lbs (1 kg) granulated sugar
½ pint (300 ml/ 1¼ cups) water
Juice of 1 lemon

Wash the damsons and put them into a saucepan with the water.

Bring to the boil and simmer for 30 minutes or until tender.

Take off the heat.

Remove the stones.

Add the sugar and lemon juice.

Return to the heat and bring to the boil again stirring to dissolve the sugar.

Boil rapidly for about 15 minutes or until setting point has been reached.

To test for setting point, put a little jam on to a cold plate. If it forms a skin that wrinkles when touched, setting point has been reached.

Pour the jam into warm, sterilized jars and cover with a circle of greaseproof paper.

When cool, seal and keep in a cool place.

PICKLED RED CABBAGE

This cabbage is traditionally served cold.

1 red cabbage
Salt
1 pint (600 ml/ 2½ cups) white malt vinegar
1 tablespoon pickling spice
1 oz (25 g) sugar
1 small beetroot

Shred the cabbage, discarding the core.

Sprinkle liberally with salt, cover and leave for 12 hours.

Put the cabbage in a colander, rinse and drain off the salt.

Pack the cabbage into large jars.

Boil the vinegar, sugar and pickling spice for about 15 minutes.

Pour over the cabbage in the jars to cover.

Slice the beetroot and put a few slices into each jar.

Seal the jars and leave for at least a week before serving.

Serve with Cumberland Tatie-Pot (see recipe).

BEAN PICKLE

Makes 3 lbs (1.5 kg)

2½ lb (1.25 kg) runner beans
2 onions
1 pint (450 ml/ 2½ cups) white wine vinegar
2 oz (50 g) flour
1 oz (25 g) mustard powder
1 teaspoon tumeric
8 oz (225 g) sugar
A little black pepper

Slice the beans and onions thinly.

Put into a saucepan and cover with water.

Bring to the boil and simmer for about 15 minutes or until tender.

Drain well.

Mix the flour, mustard powder and tumeric.

Add 2 tablespoons of the vinegar and season with a little black pepper.

Pour the remaining vinegar into a saucepan and add the flour and mustard mixture.

Heat gently, and add the sugar stirring to dissolve it.

Bring to the boil and simmer until thick.

Add the beans and onions.

Boil again for a few minutes.

Pour into warm sterilised jars and cover while still hot.

Store in a cool place until needed.

GINGER APPLES

Makes about 3 lbs (1.5 kg)

2 lbs (1 kg) cooking apples
1 lb (450 g) granulated sugar
1 pint (600 ml/ 2½ cups) water
4 oz (100 g) shredded crystallized ginger

Peel, core and quarter the apples. Keep in slightly salted water to prevent discolouration.

Boil the sugar and water in a large saucepan for 15-20 minutes.

Add the ginger and the apples.

Stew gently for a further 15-20 minutes until the apples are tender.

Turn into warm sterilised jars.

Leave to cool, seal and store in a cool place.

Serve with pork, bacon or ice-cream.

CUMBERLAND RUM BUTTER

Traditionally rum butter was made by a mother-to-be 3 months before her baby was due. It was pressed into a traditional rum butter bowl and was put under the mother's bed. When the baby was born the butter was offered to visitors on oatmeal biscuits.

A later develoment of this tradition has grown up around Braseinthwaite. Here, when the butter had been eaten and the bowl was empty it was taken by friends who filled it with gifts of money from well-wishers.

The rum butter may also be served with mince pies, Christmas pudding and other steamed puddings.

8 oz (225 g) unsalted butter
12 oz (350 g) soft brown sugar
¼ pint (150 ml/ ⅔ cup) rum
A pinch of ground cinnamon
A pinch of grated nutmeg

Cream the butter and sugar together until very soft.

Gradually add the rum and beat well.

Add the cinnamon and nutmeg.

Press into a small pot or bowl.

It will keep in a refrigerator for several weeks.

APPLE SAUCE

This sauce can be served with Cumberland Sausage. It also goes well with roast pork, duck and goose.

1 lb (450 g) cooking apples
4 tablespoons water
2 oz (50 g) soft brown sugar
Grated rind and juice of ½ lemon
A pinch of ground cloves
A pinch of grated nutmeg
1 oz (25 g) butter

Peel, core and slice the apples.

Put the apples into a saucepan with the water, the grated lemon rind, lemon juice, sugar, ground cloves and grated nutmeg.

Simmer gently until the apples are soft.

Beat in the butter.

Serve warm.

DAMSON SAUCE

This recipe comes from the area around Appleby. It is similar to Cumberland sauce and is good with venison.

8 oz (225 g) damsons
½ pint (300 ml/ 1¼ cups) port wine
3 tablespoons redcurrant jelly
1 oz (25 g) brov n sugar
A pinch of ground cinnamon
A few cloves
Juice of 1 lemon
Juice of 1 orange
1 oz (25 g) butter
A little freshly ground black pepper

Boil the damsons with the port, sugar, cinnamon and cloves for about 15 minutes.

Add the lemon and orange juice and the redcurrant jelly.

Beat well.

Remove from the heat and beat in the butter and black pepper.

Put the ingredients through a wire meshed sieve and serve.

CUMBERLAND SAUCE

This sauce is traditionally served with Cumberland ham.

6 oz (175 g) redcurrant jelly
1 level teaspoon made-up English mustard
4 tablespoons port wine
Grated rind of 1 lemon or orange

Put the redcurrant jelly, port and lemon rind into a saucepan and simmer until it has been reduced by about a quarter.

Add the mustard.

Bring to the boil again.

Serve hot or cold.

CUCUMBER SAUCE

This sauce was popular in Victorian times and was served with cold salmon.

1 cucumber
1 oz (25 g) butter
½ pint (300 ml/ 1¼ cups) single cream
2 teaspoons tarragon vingear
1 tablespoon lemon juice
A pinch of salt and pepper

Peel and slice the cucumber thinly.

Cook slowly in the butter for a few minutes.

Liquidise or rub through a wire meshed sieve and leave to cool.

Beat the cream until thick.

Mix in the tarragon vinegar and lemon juice.

Stir the cucumber purée into the cream and season with salt and pepper.

SLOE GIN

3 pints (1.75 litres) sloes
3 pints (1.75 litres) gin
1 lb (450 g) sugar
A few bitter almonds

Wash and prick the sloes with a needle.

Layer the sloes in large sterilized jars with the sugar, until each jar is three-quarters full.

Fill the jars with gin and seal tightly.

Leave for 8 weeks, shaking occasionally.

Strain and bottle.

Vintner

DAMSON GIN

2 lbs (1 kg) damsons
1½ lb (675 g) granulated sugar
Gin — about 4 pints (2.25 litres)

Wash the damsons and prick each one with a needle.

Layer the fruit and sugar in large preserving jars until the jars are half full.

Fill the jars with gin.

Seal tightly.

Leave in a cool place for at least 12 weeks, shaking the jars occasionally.

Filter into bottles.

The gin improves with age.

a Tipler

For the Sting of a Wasp in the Throte

Take some honey and sweet oil with a little vinegar and with a spoon beat them well together in a half pint basin to be continually taking some of it till the pain is abated.

A Cure for a Cold

Take 1 handful of hoarhound put it in two quarts of water, boil it down to one half, then strain it, put in some honey, put it on a fire to incorporate, then add a little old rum, and cork it up. Take half a teaspoonful in a cupful of warm milk, fasting, and another about noon, on an empty stomach.

Acknowlegements:

Grateful thanks are extended to the many people of Cumberland and Westmorland who have contributed towards this collection of recipes, including:

The Cumbria Records Office, Kendal, for Cure for a Cold and For the Sting of A Wasp in the Throte (Ref. WDX 211).

Joan Hebson of Cockermouth for information about Rum Butter.

THE COUNTRY RECIPE SERIES

Available now @ £1.95 each

Cambridgeshire
Cornwall
Cumberland & Westmorland
Devon
Dorset
Hampshire
Kent
Lancashire
Norfolk
Somerset
Sussex
Yorkshire

Coming September 1988

Leicestershire
Oxfordshire
Suffolk
Warwickshire

All these books are available at your local bookshop or newsagent, or can be ordered direct from the publisher. Just tick the titles you require and fill in the form below. Prices and availability subject to change without notice.

Ravette Books Limited, 3 Glenside Estate, Star Road, Partridge Green, Horsham, West Sussex RH13 8RA.

Please send a cheque or postal order, and allow the following for postage and packing. UK 25p for one book and 10p for each additional book ordered.

Name ....

Address..

....

....